Collection of Flaws in a Black Dress

poems by

Jenny Williamson

Finishing Line Press
Georgetown, Kentucky

Collection of Flaws
in a Black Dress

ACKNOWLEDGMENTS

Thank you to Sara Eileen Hames. Without you, this wouldn't exist.

Thank you to Brittney Canty. All good ideas flow from you.

Thank you to David Dyte and Emily Lubanko, and to the 24cc community. Your
talent knows no bounds.

Thank you to Genn McMenemy Stone, Jordana Frankel, Amy Williamson, Sam
Williamson, Steven Padnick, Lynsey Griswold, Jayel Draco, Angela Garenani
Marshall, and Minet AB Marrin Fischer. For everything.

Thank you to Mary Hussmann, for the encouragement and patient teaching.

Thank you to everyone who contributed to my Kickstarter. You are deeply
appreciated.

And thank you to Tom and Linda Williamson, always.

Publisher: Leah Maines
Editor: Christen Kincaid
Cover Art: Emily Lubanko
Author Photo: David Dyte
Cover Design: Elizabeth Maines

Printed in the USA on acid-free paper.
Order online: www.finishinglinepress.com
also available on amazon.com

Author inquiries and mail orders:
Finishing Line Press
P. O. Box 1626
Georgetown, Kentucky 40324
U. S. A.

Table of Contents

For Jack

Possibility

I touched my tongue to the place at the root of your throat
and fell like a planet around a star.

A thunderstorm built in my body. Archipelago of lightning;
half-moon rising under my skin.

You put your hands on me.
I put all of my bones in one basket

and followed you five continents, a litany of yes
sweating into the mattress.

When the time comes for you to break me
use more than your words.

Use your mouth and your breath.
Use your own two hands.

Inner Space

Spread me open like a book;
a universe turned outside-in.

Galaxies spin out their filmy webs
under my skin; my heart a pulsing quasar,
blazing metronome of light.

I tell you this so you'll understand
the distance I've traveled to find you.

On the days when my words must navigate an uncountable vastness
where there can be no language,
I watch for what you are:

a touch so close it breathes
as lungs do.

Binary System

It was the distance you loved,
and the way I wore it—
a slip-shouldered dress
I would take off and on
just as easy as going.

It was a look that flattered me.
For once in my life I was not too much;
I was only enough.

On the day I first spun you
into my bed, you folded in on me
like a collapsing star.

These days we circle each other,
always receding, even when drawing near;
speaking *I love you* in so many languages
but never *stay*.

This Desert

We are just like each other, two bags of skin
full of blood and fireworks.

My love, where have you gone?
On an eternal quest for cigarettes
at the corner store

walking through a desert of your own devising,
trailing behind you the tattered names
of all your past lovers.

Write me the story of where you've been.
Write it in fire with thirsty footprints
then open your umbrella and call for rain.

I am the deluge you've been searching for,
fluid right down to my shame.

Press me and I bend for you.
Touch me and I come off
on your hands.

Suicide Love Letter

Stay. The world is bright as citrus
today and I made you your favorite dish
and nothing can possibly go wrong,
even the things that do.

Stay. I am wearing a new dress and I
have painted a new and better
face on my face for you.

Stay. There is music in the city.
There is a far-off song shimmering over the city
and the day is hopeful as green grass.
The day is an open door.

Stay. Just for a minute.
Just long enough to see the sun
break itself on the back of this river.

Stay. I have scraped all this holy light
off the cobblestones of every street
where you ever held my hand.

If I could I would give it all back to you.
If I could I would love the black hole
right out of your chest.

Terminal 8

I have carved on my palm the number of times you have left me
standing on windy train platforms, in airport atriums
just before the security line.

Between us a tender filament
stretched long over the tossing Atlantic.
We tried to drift easy in the shallow places
but lover, I float like a freight train.

I love you refused to be quiet;
It pushed itself out of me.
You asked me what is love, really.

Used the passive voice
as if I didn't know the difference.
On the last day I laid down

to watch the sun break open and spill across your chest.
Your body was only a temporary refuge.

When you finally passed through airport security,
they looked at you like they always do—
like there's something you're not telling.

Listen. You don't need me to tell you what love is.
You feel it open its wings in your throat
every time you watch me wave goodbye.

What's Yours Is Mine

I am not myself. I am a haunted house
full of ghastly furniture.
You gather me up in your arms—

I see you. I see you suffer.
I feel very seen.

I am not myself. I am a collection of flaws
in a black dress. Finish your memoir;
name me the villain.

One day you will finish mapping the topography of our sorrow
and you will see there is only one road
leading out.

On that day, do not blame me
for what you do.
Blame the collection of flaws
in the mirror.

Bury

Outside the window the night sky
is being dramatic;
starving galaxies eating their own.

This hunger I know the name of.
The desire to open my arms
to the avalanche; to gather you in

all *momentum* and *mori*.
Instead I press my love into the ground
with a face full of blood and
vomit in its hair.

Where will it go, after?
It would not be the first thing
ever to rise from the dead.

You've done it yourself more than once;
taught yourself how to die and come back
between eye-blinks
without anyone knowing.

Slow Fade

I am leaving you by inches.
Already I am insubstantial as a jellyfish.
The slightest of currents undoes me.

Someday I may rest.
Someday I may curl myself around
this wound and sleep.

Pont des Arts

The iron bridge is burning. Apocalypse
of love locks. Not even an avalanche of river—

not even you can pull me from the water
this time. All this time
I have carried the ending in my body.

You will look at me in such a way
as to tell me I am not beautiful now
but I will be, in retrospect.

I will tell you I am sorry
for my weeping unlovable self
and you will say water
under the bridge

and both of us will watch this river
bury itself beneath our feet;
both turning our faces away

from this bomb
in my chest, this detonator
in your fist.

Kitchen Wound

When the knife slipped, my skin parted
easy as a curtain.
I used to trust my body not to bleed.

Warm red starburst hot on my tongue;
flush of shame in my mouth.

Now a long fearsome numbness
streaks up the inside of my finger.
Another part of me departed.
I did it to myself.

Under my skin, an invisible map
of the parts of me I've lost,
all the ways I'd deserved
to be left.

come back to me   come back
I can be better.

Necropolis

At night my heart is a box of bees
and I can't sleep.

In the morning the city has birthed
a new self, pink and squalling
every nerve exposed.

I go for a walk on a nameless street.
The white crane inside me unfolds its wings
and beats itself bloody against my breastbone.
The catcallers all hide their faces.

It takes me days to find the place
where the tombstones still bloom.
Every night I come here

and dig up your grave.
In the morning I bury you.

Men on the Corner

My street is a patchwork of potholes
full of strange rainwater.
The man on the corner purses his lips at me,

calls me beautiful. A ghost in his face that I recognize.
On the days when the teeth of the city chew the horizon
this is where they wait for me.

To get by I must push past the weight
of their wanting.

To them I must seem soft as fruit-flesh—
skin to split with their fingers;
seeds to thumb out onto the ground.

The Distance Between Me
and Other People, Always

She wears a scarlet dress.
On particularly blessed occasions
I catch glimpses of her
in far-off mirrors, a gregarious prism
busy dividing the light.

No granted wish will make me this woman.
The story I'm telling is long-winded and
awkwardly spun,
of value to no one. Reliably tone-deaf,
I do not know it
until the brittle pause at the end.

The people glance away, reach for their wine glasses,
wrist-bones clinking against the light
from the jagged chandelier.
I fold, bird-shouldered, back
into every empty pause, each tiny
conversational betrayal.

The woman in the mirror curves her mouth
in flawless exchange,
a luminous scarf draping itself
across her vivid collarbones.

It is moments like this when I feel her the most:
so close to me; so unforgivably far.

Ocean in my Bed

This man is a boy is a man
is a jumpy electron under my tongue.
He scales walls; he is unafraid
of altered states.

We go to work on this joint
venture of our pleasure.
Our backs strain together.
We pound it into the ground.

In my arms he holds back and holds back and holds
everything back
until I spill over; a deluge I never consented to give—but here
it is. Here
I am.

Afterwards I do not speak. I am only
a worn nub.
There is a vast distance of unshared history.

It pulses between us, this ocean—
a body with no maps
or moorings.

Stargazer

I have waited for you in my black dress.
I have ground up these bones for your coffee.
Goddammit I said I was sorry

but an apology is not an airplane.
Without fail, whenever I wish for you

what I get is this bar, the color of flesh and neon
and a different love each night—
an endless parade of not-you.

You swore you would take me to Paris
where you would love me good and well
til my heart was a poor dead thing
bleeding out on the floorboards.

How can I refuse?
Before you go for good, I wish you
would bring me a cup of that sorry

and press your hand to the place
where my hope is, dumb unblinking telescope
pointed at sky.

Sylvie

The day that I learned her name
was the day I saw my life laid at my feet
like some kind of unspeakable highway.

A nighttime eulogy. An unrest that swallows itself.
I am the owl that haunts these ruins.

When will I see you again?
I keep coming back to a sea full of lions;
a hand that I clung to once.

Retrace our path across continents. Retrace it
with whomever you like.
Remind me we made no promises.

Look at me, poor thing. Staring and staring.
The shadows build up in her dark hair
until even I cannot fathom her face.

Rue du Chemin Vert

Someone has stripped the skin from the street where we used to live.
The tatters hang over the neck of this lamppost,
dripping light.

Perhaps it is some kind of sacrifice.
A life offering for tired bees.

It is raining in the city you chose
to be alone in. A pall of mist
that suffocates the rooftops

and collects under the eaves of the old apartment.
Even then I knew

about the town beneath your skin where it always rains
and the roads all go to the same dark place.

It has been so long since your body
has spoken its truth to my body,

spinning together the story
of after. It was not true, of course—

no afterlife is—but it was everything I wanted.

This moon-skin street, this story
that left us both.

Photograph of a Burning City

I wanted a candid photo,
less than photogenic, more real than real.

It showed me a horizon full of teeth marks.
It showed me a drowned carousel.
It showed me a shipwreck leaning

down Second Avenue,
boarded and shut.

My photo at last was of myself
sunken-cheeked and transformed.
I never planned to become
what the city has made me.

Never thought its uncanny
could wear on me so easy.

Life Story

I walked into the year machine
in the season of fallen leaves.

The years passed in cycles of seven;
my breastbone emerged from my chest
like the prow of a ship.

My lovers all had shoulders that spoke
like an orchestra; shoulders that shut
my mouth.

I never had a child
but some days solace turned in my womb
like a promise.

I lived a life hemmed in by mysteries.
I made a blanket of my solitude.
I learned how to keep myself warm.

There was a road. I chose it.
There was a door. I opened it.
I loved and I loved.

Permian Extinction

It was the Conodonts that went first.
Long soft sea-ribbons,
unlikely predators with their lateral eyes
and unexpected teeth.

Then the Orthida, already ancient,
stoic and single-valved
spinning their war stories of the Pre-Cambrian.

No one expected the Bryozoa to hold on
as long as they did.
Crowned in showy tentacles,
they came in a cacophony of shapes
dancing invertebrate showponies
doomed as dinner.

Long before our oldest ancestors
mud-puppied onto the beaches
with the sea in their wombs

the ocean swallowed its stillbirths
and kept its secrets.

Vision Quest

Wheat fields and mud fields and grass and bones
under a panoply of planets; in this world
even the most blameless meadow
hides an invisible desert.

I am an insatiable being.
Bring me a strand of pearls
and a bright pink lipstain
and a pop of lavender to flatter the eye

or I'll cut it all off at the root.
Just like the people who cushioned the meteor
and the poor doomed buffalo
and the goldfish I flushed in the fifth grade.

I have put on the world-colored glasses.
I have come through the green and the static.
Now I can't see through all this rain.

What is the sum of this life?
It is the universe in all of us.
It is the road we will die on.

In the Room

It is more than a shadow over my face.
It is my own skull rising out of my skin
in slow motion;
the years piled up in the yard like slaughtered wolves.

Sometimes I catch my death
in the corner of my left eye
and trap it behind a contact lens.

It is a thing I have learned to live with,
like migraines,
or a penchant for choosing wrong.

In the last room, I want it to be you.
Bring me a bouquet of lightning and pussywillow
and all you ever were, in manuscript form.

I will be the old woman
clasping the limp word-corpse of my own life story
close to my chest, the smoke of my last burnt offering
rising from my mouth.

Trepanation

When I woke they'd put a doorway
in my skull
round as a bone moon.

The ghosts gnawed through me, trailing
a terrible howling.

It was not painful. Quite the opposite,
this hole in the hull of my ship
rimmed with stars—

I could no longer tell where I ended
and the sky began.

Resurrect

In the last days the rogue planet
swung low and fat on the horizon.

We had watched it come for years,
the cities devouring themselves in the dark.

We put a name to our own undoing.
We collided as orbit demanded,

so hard our cores were made to merge.
The moon was ripped from my belly.

Later the green algae will come
and breathe the atmosphere into existence.

Later the trilobytes and dinosaurs;
the terror birds and smilodons.

Now is the season of drowned mountaintops
and sulfur skies. Look for me; I am not dead.

I will be here, sleeping
among the seeds.

Pole Vault

If time is a wishbone, then death must be a great big room
where all you have lost is returned to you.

I wanted to be a pole vault. Not the vaulter but the pole,
planted on earth, made to bend

not for the great cosmic sieve
that keeps our dear departed souls
from falling into the sky;
but because this is what I was made for.

I have shouldered my earthly pain all the bleeding miles
to Bethlehem;
I have bent my back to the business of grief.

Now I would choose to stand here
on the edge of this cliff face—
joy unfolding in my heart
like a child's inflatable bouncy castle.

I am forgiven. I have forgiven myself.

J enny Williamson writes primarily about sex and death. She is published in journals including *East Coast Literary Review, Burningwood Literary Journal,* and *Vox Poetica.* She is also an actress and fiction writer, and currently lives in Brooklyn. This is not her last chapbook.

More information can be found at www.JennyWilliamson.net.

www.ingramcontent.com/pod-product-compliance
Lightning Source LLC
LaVergne TN
LVHW041329080426
835513LV00008B/650